# 7 Ways to Succeed In Winning Friends

*An Easy Way to Communicate, Impress, Be Enthusiastic and Connect With People for a Fulfilling Life*

Sneha Rajput

# Contents

# INTRODUCTION

This book aims to make the reader aware of various aspects of life to succeed in winning friends. The acquisition of knowledge to develop friendly relations is another objective. One can, with perception and intuition, apply steps to win friends. Read on to learn more about simple changes in life to successfully win friends. The purpose of this book is simple and effective. This is a practical, manual for action to personal improvement.

Read this book carefully, thoughtfully, absorbing its teachings. I have designed the '7 Ways to Succeed in Winning friends' for millions of people to connect with others in any age group. If you sincerely follow the ways set forth, you can experience an amazing improvement in yourself. It offers you creative strategies to get a renewable resource of friends to drive away your loneliness. The reader will be happy to get out of some daily difficult circumstances. Friends are a necessity of life. You will have an expanded friend circle. This book will benefit people to change their attitude towards life. Enjoy a larger friend circle on implementing the ideas put up, allowing the reader to lead a happy daily life.

# CHAPTER 1 Activate a feeling of importance in the other person

"I judge people by their own principles, not my own."

Martin Luther King

A friend is of ample support and a resource of power. A friend is a secret direction to your vision to achieve your goals in life and give thoughts to your pattern. Talk to people frankly. Have profound interactions to get the best out of your talks with them. Clarify and strengthen your thoughts to attract people to befriend you. Friends improve health, as they are close to developing a feeling of importance. Think in terms of other people, rather than having your fixed perspective. That will help one to be recognized for importance.

It is human nature to be happy about getting recognition even in trivial matters. The feeling of being important is pleasing to comfort the well being. The one who makes us feel important, we get connected soon and remember him for that good turn. Interest the people in your work, by making them feel important. Arouse their curiosity in a topic of discussion that they like. This is one of the best investments one can do to get closer and connect to people.

Theodore Roosevelt revealed that the royal road to a person's heart is through talking about the things he treasures the most.

## Arouse a feeling of importance

As I write this chapter, I remember a story my granny once told me. Raman, a school teacher, wanted some help for his project from an entrepreneur. Raman approached him with a scheduled time fixed for the meeting. Being an eminent industrialist, he gave Raman ten valuable minutes of his time. The businessman first greeted Raman to start the conversation. He asked the teacher to translate an English proverb 'Time is money'. Raman felt elated, as this man wanted to learn something in his mother tongue. Such a feeling of being important takes one to the seventh heaven. Raman treasured the interaction in his heart. He began to like and buy all articles manufactured by this business owner's firm and propagated their sale.

I remember in school and Junior college days, I participated in many competitions. They were the inter-house debate, sports, elocution, poetry recitation, calligraphy, etc. Some sports like basketball, I participated at the district and state levels. I received gold and silver medals for the running race too besides trophies for the other competitions. My mother made a big rack in our house to display the medals and trophies that I had won in school. Whenever any relative or a guest visited us, my mother made it an event to display them. She showed the medals and trophies to all. She praised me lavishly for my achievement and narrated details to the visitors. Some people were quite interested and thought of inspiring their children to participate in competitions. Guests praised me for my work. Some were least bothered about it. My mother continued this without a second thought. She always made me feel important and gave a different identity to a girl child. I eagerly waited for this event at the arrival of guests. I never dared to ask her why she did this, but as time passed I grew up to realize the feeling of importance she aroused in me. This built my confidence.

Shelly, my neighbor, the owner of a travel agency once reported: "I was shocked to hear about Dolly, who was as much a friend as an employee, submitted her resignation letter. I cared for her, and never criticized her work. I somehow could not accept her resignation. In front of all others in the office, I had remarked, "What a great deal you mean for this company? I see no reason for your resignation". I took Dolly out to a restaurant of her choice and discussed the whole matter. I talked to her about her family, her hobbies, her passion, and made her feel comfortable for hours together. She withdrew her resignation letter. She was happy to get the importance she was craving for."

People enjoy it if you talk about them, their family, their children's achievements, and the core world around them. They love to prioritize themselves along with their family.

I was in the bank waiting for my turn for the fixed deposit signature. It was very quiet there, except the fans that churned incessantly. All people were busy with computers at their desks. When it was my turn, I just praised the lady's braided hair with a fragrant red rose in it. I said, "I wish I had beautiful long hair like you". She blushed and replied, "Many people like my long hair. Thank you for the compliment". There was no selfish motive in this praise. I didn't want anything out of this. It was just a simple effort to cheer her up. I'm sure she might have shared this with her family members, the importance bestowed upon her. The unexpected compliment in the daily work environment can give pleasure for the rest of the day.  She might've looked at her hair for a long time, with all thoughts of caring for them.

Mr. Peterson was an eminent entrepreneur controlling many business companies. He regularly interviewed youngsters to employ for his firms.  He took pleasure in this duty. He searched efficient people with knowledge and skills for his firms. One afternoon as he was busy with his work, the weather suddenly changed. There was a mix of summer showers in the sunlit hours. A young man drenched in clean rainwater entered for the interview. Mr. Peterson was annoyed to see him enter. He was startled at the youngster's words, "I will make money for you and your company in these many ways". He explained all ways that made Mr. Peterson feel the importance of a successful man. He got a vision to make his firms successful internationally. Multiple ways were assured along with significant cost-cutting.

He was impressed and he employed the person. His business prospered.

## Simplicity

A simple way in your work and life makes many follow you. They are attracted to your simple daily life and like to befriend you. It can be as simple as helping an unknown.

Mother Teresa was once asked by interviewers, "What do you get in going down the lanes in Calcutta with a lot of filth and poverty to see?" Mother Teresa had a beautiful answer, "I find Jesus Christ in every child I serve in the streets of Calcutta". She always showed simplicity in the great work she did. She did not expect anything in return from those she served. Many people from all over the world followed her. Today we find her work of helping others going on through a mission. Express kindness, care, love, and beauty to expand beneficial results in seeking friendship.

Ralph Waldo Emerson said, "Love is our highest word and a synonym for God".

Talk about a person's children. Beautiful thoughts build a beautiful soul. Praise their good deeds. A small speech delivered by a child in school, a first-time job of a teenager, a cake baked, a melodious song sung by a child, etc. Talk about their education, work, or creativity. You may also try to solve a person's problems selflessly. One day as I was traveling home from the office, I just peeped in a friend's house on my way. It was the birthday of one of her daughters. I opened the cover of the box in which I had carried a cake for my kids. The girl was delighted to see me bring her a cake to celebrate her birthday. It was a surprise for her. I handed the cake to her. I thought I could buy another one for my kids. The happiness on the girl's face was a pleasure to watch. She began calling me 'Cake aunty' since then. Small deeds make people so happy and cherish the important feeling.

## Make one feel popular

Once a guest for a school function asked children, "What do you want the most in your life?" There were multiple answers such as money, highest marks, good clothes, shoes, delicacies to relish, etc.  However, the most common answer given was - to be popular in society. Elderly people also want to be popular. If you deliberately try to be popular, you may not get what you desire. Try to be the one where people discuss your uniqueness. When you pass by people will say, "He has something that he can give others." Start with your precious smile. Speak to others about the smallest help one has given you, for example, the first aid when you slipped and scraped your knee, a collection of data on your computer, help with assembling your work, tips on filing documents, support in making small videos, lending you some articles, etc. Tell goodness done to you to others so that your benefactor has a feeling of popularity in the right sense.  That makes one an important personality. Try to bring out the inner talent in others. She can sing a song in a group of people, play a musical note, and sketch in a few minutes. The person will feel popular and seek your help for the same, and approach you in a very friendly manner.

Let go of small things, so that people start liking you. Show your willingness to express others' popularity. Small acts of letting go of differences of opinion that could create future quarrels are important steps towards gaining popularity. This is a powerful tool to take you towards popularity by making others feel happy. Keep your emotions aside, and let go of trivial things, so you move on to positivity. Otherwise negative emotions start making you weak. Such thoughts haunt your well-being. Positive thoughts will make you strong in every challenge you face.

First, become a comfortable person whom people enjoy meeting. In the mornings, the first person you see other than your family is the sweeper of the building. You just wish him a simple 'Good Morning'. This has come to you quite mechanically as a part of your daily routine. Stop by to talk to him someday and inquire about his family. Discuss his interest in various topics. This will establish friendly relations that you may not have thought of before. Interact with the milkman, the newspaper boy, the garbage picking van driver, etc. and find out how they fare during any crisis they face. Do not hesitate while you interact with them. They will wait for your arrival, to see you smile at them. They will turn out to be the biggest aid during any difficulty. You make them feel important with your daily conversations with them. They find a friend in you.

Anne talks to the maids who work for her, the gardener who visits to weed out and trim her plants. She shows concern for them. Anne often remarks, "It's a sunny morning, clear weather". Her words make the helping visitor, the gardener, the maid feel important. She also shares tea or sandwiches once in a while. People do appreciate little warm gestures, often reciprocate generously, but most importantly, always remember them. The maid and the gardener often work long hours at Anne's place, and with utmost attention, as if it's their own.

In this chapter, you read about my concept of various ways we can make one feel important. The activation of this emotion in others can be through simplicity, care, and hospitality you show to them. The simplicity in your act of kindness, the way you make others feel popular, the importance you give a person with a small morning good wish, the positivity in your mind to instigate a feeling of importance in others – all these can go long way building relationships.

You can put this message in chapter one, into practice in your daily life intentionally. In the next chapter, you will read how to reveal your nature through simple thoughts. Connect to others through links.

# Chapter 2   Respect the Personality of an Individual

Thoughts reveal your divine nature.


I know, under this heaven, if you want to get anything done for you, it is to have pleasing respectable words from others.

One story that is traditionally told in every Indian house, is that about Lord Shri Krishna's friendship with Sudama. Sudama was Lord Krishna's childhood friend. He was poor and hardly had food to eat. One day his wife suggested going to his friend Lord Krishna, who was rich and well respected by society. She said, "Ask your friend to help you." Sudama decided to meet Krishna, his dear friend. The day arrived, Sudama dressed to leave for a delightful visit. His wife gave him some poha, an Indian snack made from puffed rice. After a long journey, Sudama reached the palace of Lord Krishna. Seeing his beggarly state, the palace guards enquired about him. He politely replied, "I have come to meet Shri Krishna". He was led into the palace to Shri Krishna. Shri Krishna was happy to meet his childhood friend. He asked, "What have you brought for me, my dear friend?" Sudama hesitantly took out a small cloth bag, opened it, and spread it out with the poha. Krishna enjoyed the delicious poha brought for him. The court was astonished to see

Krishna eat the Poha brought for him. When Sudama returned home, he saw a beautiful house where his wife was waiting for him.

Greet the supporting staff from the school of your child whenever you visit the school for any meeting; though they may not be well educated, they do serve the school and take care of your child during school hours. It is them who would help your child whenever he falls and hurts his knee, take him to the basin if vomiting, or cleans it. Your 'good morning' makes their day. They get a good feeling. You are respecting the person and the work he or she is doing. You show dignity for all work.

Mr. Moore daily went around in his company. He interacted with the supporting staff daily, only to boost them with happiness, and a feeling of being respected. On his way, he would say, "Hey Lily, good morning, I am happy to see you work so hard. Hello Robin, how is your work?" He had a wish for all his maids and workers. They waited for the boss to come to wish them, be it morning or evening. They worked as if cleaning their own house. There was hardly any undue absenteeism.

We feed the body with delicacies prepared for every festival, party, meeting but we forget to feed the mind. We hardly think of the needs of a person's mind to be mentally free of stress. This can be done by a small 'hello' to an employee on your way in the company or passing by the house. Proceed to produce happiness among the masses. Make it a routine to be happy and spread happiness. Wear a broad smile on your face at the sight of someone to make him feel important. Forget self and think of others.

Theodore Roosevelt with his great willingness always said 'hello' to all on his way, he always had good words for all workers. This raised their enthusiasm to work. People remembered this great person throughout.


**Think and act for yourself**

Ronny, a rich boy in my neighborhood, went down the streets every Sunday at 9 am to help senior citizens. He served the beggars, helped the blind to go down the street to reach the park. He had a lot of respect for every individual. He dressed their wounds, gave them a healthy breakfast with entertainment on his guitar. I call this unconditional friendship. His idea was followed by many young boys and he became quite popular in the neighborhood and among teenagers. Some people do not think of others, as they are involved in their own worries. They are not interested in anything else, as their personal life is their only concern. Let your personality be such that people will like to see you daily.

In college, there are boys, where the bonding is over alcohol. These boys go out to get drunk regularly. They avoid classes or going to the library, are arrogant, and bully the weak. Dramatize to them individually, the bad effects of their habits. One to one correspondence can very effectively change this habit. Do avoid criticizing this habit. The root cause is the mindset that has to be changed. Divert them with positivity to your way of life. The confidence in them will help overcome withdrawal symptoms. Distract the flock of bad birds to save your friend. This act needs a very thoughtful mind.

Develop such habits that people start liking you. The youngsters going to the college library to read books, study, make notes, help the librarian, etc. Make a unit of the readers in the library. Perform some tasks that are difficult for others. Exchange your ideas about the books that you read with others. Respect the view of the reader though it may not be your niche. Initiate conversation politely and softly after library hours. Reading improves your intellectual value. You would be able to discuss any topic in this world. You will certainly learn a lot of strategies from fellow readers. Your presence will be awaited as they have accepted you as a friend soon. You will be a source of motivation for all. Think and you will have a source to acquire friends in every nook and corner of life. The selection of friends is the inspiration from within.

Express gratitude to all which shows respect. There was a coaching class where students received their science and math lessons regularly. Parents had paid the required amount as fees. The tutor was teaching with lots of effort and enthusiasm. It was the right of the students to get their queries resolved. A student thanked the tutor every time her query was answered. The tutor felt good for the gratitude expressed.

Her habit was soon inculcated by others to thank the tutor and develop friendliness with the tutor who felt respected.  Gratitude makes the other person feel good and receives respect.

A professor working in a college always thanked the peons for every little bit of work. All the fellow professors mocked her for this act. She continued without paying any heed to this. She valued every little help from others. This surprised the peons, who felt overwhelmed at the thought of a highly qualified person always thanks them, while they were just doing their duties. All working in an institute perform their duty. Yet you make a little effort to thank one, it makes a lot of difference.

In the village where I spent my childhood, there was a lady. She asked small children to help her. She wanted a glass of water, latch windows, collect books, and arrange racks. She expressed gratitude to them. All were astonished at her as they felt it the duty of the children to help her. The children always willingly helped her. They were impressed with her as she was very thankful to the children. The practice of elderly people accepting help from youngers with gratitude got embedded fixed in their minds.

## Do not criticize

Hans Selye, a great psychologist said, "As much we thirst for approval, we dread condemnation."

In India, there is a state of rich cultural heritage, Rajasthan.  There is a story about it. In this state, there is a small village with just about five hundred population. It is believed that people do not cut trees there. If they want to remove a tree from that place if it obstructs any development or construction work, villagers gather around the tree and criticize it. They curse it loudly. They then return home for daily chores. No one for the rest of the day goes to that tree. The act goes on daily for nearly a week. The tree starts withering. It dries up. Even plants have emotions. Criticism demoralizes a living thing. Never criticize anyone as it demoralizes. It leaves the hope of survival.

A father always compared his son with other children from the neighborhood. He told his son he was not good at impressing others. He was weak at studies. He was not bold.  This demoralized the child. He could hardly do anything as he lost all his confidence. He never thought of rising to work, earn, or lead a good life. He was unable to handle his father's business. At the age of twenty-eight, he was declared unsuccessful. He didn't want to visit relatives and friends and started avoiding people at functions. He would enjoy with the drivers and the supporting staff, but could not rise as a confident person to do any work on his own. Do not criticize anyone. People become weak in condemnation.

If you criticize anyone, it hurts the pride and makes that person feel unimportant.

Scolding children, employees, or colleagues for a small mistake will reduce their interest in work. Such temperament may develop due to worries over any financial situation. Avoid complaining about their work. They may understand their job a little slowly. Their analysis of the problem may be suboptimal than what you expect from them. Criticizing does not help in improving the work or the attitude of the person. Before criticism try to find circumstances in which the person may be stuck up. First of all, try to keep yourself in his position to understand his reality. We deal with people so activate their emotional motivation.

We speak with the view of our choice. One may dislike the arrangement of the living room of a person one visits. Criticism begins. One may dislike the decoration for a function or marriage. We visualize it to be our way. In a group, we begin with the envious mind that never leaves us at such times. It rules us; the lavish expenses brighten our eyes. This is as one cannot accept the beauty or the expenditure. You envy the riches of the host. Throw away negative feelings from your mind. Negative thoughts lead you to criticism. To befriend someone, drop petty issues from your mind. They don't gain anything other than criticism. It keeps you away from your friends.

It is very easy to be a critic. Finding faults with others is quite simple. We start expressing ourselves without the thought of others. Do not try to see the other side of the coin. Express without a second thought. Plants and animals too cannot accept criticism. All stay safe from critics, avoid their company. Criticism comes to mind due to petty issues. One cannot achieve the level of success starts criticism.

As I conclude this chapter I would like to remind you to throw away this self-imposed obstacle of your three-lettered word 'ego'. So respect the individual before you, irrespective of his riches or position in society. Know that you have the power to control your habits to be receptive of a personality. Further, we will discuss how acceptance for you comes from all walks of society. Your ability to be authentic will motivate others. Awaken the minds to join you.

## CHAPTER 3 Your Presence Inspires Others

"Always be yourself and have faith in yourself. Do not go out and look for a successful personality and try to duplicate it."

Bruce Lee

You need friends to share your feelings. Smile as soon as you see a person in front of you. A smile says, "I'm glad to see you. You made my day.  You made me happy." Be determined to stand by the achievement of people. Let them find comfort in your company. Life is strange and quite happy. Success has many friends around it, while failure has none. Be genuine in your work; let authenticity be the gem you carry for inspiring others. They will be attracted to the authentic behavior you show. You can inspire a prosperous friendship. Your dreams come true if you find friends like you. Birds of a feather flock together. You share the same thoughts, views to agree soon.  They will help creativity and constructive life to succeed. False and flashy attractions are short-lived. Try to identify such friends. Some cater to only financial status. They are with you to enjoy your money and amenities.

## Caring attitude

Some students stayed in a hostel. A senior was ill, suffered from loose motions. Surekha always had some admiration for this senior. Reena was a very friendly girl.  She was kind to all. Surekha thought this was the best time to get close to know Reena. So she made decoction using coffee and lime. "Have this, you will get relief," she said to Reena. In the evening she came with the second dose and sat by her side to massage her feet, talk to her. Surekha prayed for the recovery of her ill friend. Reena was happy to find a new friend so caring and helpful. Reena never knew this Surekha who now got added to her friend list. Nurture a relation with efforts to be friendly. This can be a special bond to hold you together. Your true nature is revealed through such help. You are a true person to help during others' illnesses.

A school pedagogue lost his job, did not find any other source of income. He was the only breadwinner for the family. The savings were getting over. Stress and fear started mounting. How to feed the family? The concern made him guilty, and frustration rose. Expenses started mounting with the electricity bill, house rent, grocer's bill, paper bill, etc. He made an appeal to colleagues for help. One good man rushed in to help the pedagogue and settled all his bills. The pedagogue returned the amount as soon as he received his pay from a new job. The attitude to help others during a crisis makes good friends. You will gain happiness and friends with this help.

Parents should bestow caring towards children in the puberty period. I would like to mention this lacuna in society, especially in developing countries. This is the time when the child needs a lot of friendly help from parents. A father can be a very good friend of the son; and a mother, the best friend of her daughter. Both can shoulder the responsibility of growing children. Show that you do care. Talk about your experiences with your child. Make him comfortable. Let him express himself. Speak to the child as you spoke to your school friend. Generate such confidence that he tells you everything like a friend. The girl can tell you daily happenings in her school, on the playground, hobby class, etc. Spare quality time for the special interaction of the day, where the family sits together to express. Listen to every even and odd of the child. Talk about your day to them. Enjoy jokes in life. Bake a pizza or a cake with their help. Explain to them the meanings of simple words, help them with studies, and solve their problems. This will stop them from getting into bad company or getting attracted to addiction. If you are very busy with your work, schedule sometime of your day to spare even if just ten minutes for your kids. Try learning something new from your child, as simple as the way she waters the garden, knits a new knot, sings a verse, chants a mantra, does a new exercise, etc. Go along with them for a morning jog, play cricket, discuss the latest happenings in the world, join a gymkhana together. Your child will wait for the moment daily longing to meet this friend. You can be the best friend of your child.

## Make an Assumption of friendship

If others can do it I can as well. Start acting accordingly. If you are a shy person the assumption of making friends will effectively help you. Assume you are a very popular person with a big circle of friends around you to cater to your needs. It gives you a satisfactory feeling. You are the hero of the movie strolling with a crowd. Bring this assumption to reality. Do not fear to attempt. Let the traitor's doubts go away from your mind. Strengthen your will power to get friends. Follow the tips I have mentioned in this book. Write them down in a diary as soon as you wake up in the morning. Try different ways one by one. Don't mix all, as too many cooks spoil the broth. Read and implement them once a week. It takes twenty-one days to form a habit which becomes a lifestyle within ninety days. Friends, go for it. Show that you care for them and motivate them. You can be an inspiration for many.

## Be an Optimist

Optimists have faith and hope in every action. Be optimistic in every small action daily. Have a good reason to wake up in the morning hoping to make a new friend. They shape the course and identity of our life. Learn optimism. Search reasons for optimism. You are the one to live to vibrate the energy of optimism so that people will willingly accompany you. Attempt to anticipate what would make your friend happy and fulfilled. You have to take great ideas for the action of completion. All enjoy the company of an action hero. Accept change, as it makes you leave your earlier routine to add something new to bring out a better version of you. Think of a problem as an opportunity. Release and develop your potential ideas to help others financially. A boy in school days was just to the mark in studies, hardly had any friends. He had high potential. I recently met him. Now he has achieved the position of a higher level officer. I asked, "How did you achieve this?" He replied, "I had hope, that helped me gather friends. I tried to change my situation with education. The commitment to befriend - they loved my optimistic nature. I had all the honest and loyal friends.  My poverty was an exception. They helped me financially. They collected the amount for the enrolment of the test to achieve this post. I put in my heart towards my studies to prove to my friends. That was the best return gift I could give my friends. That's all." His words still ring in my ears.

Your presence inspires others to greatness, good health, beauty, and allows them to feel the uniqueness of your personality. They feel energetic about your presence. Instill confidence in them, to become their better versions. You leave a positive impact on others.


## Call by the first name

The name is a very pleasing sound that one knows. It is always good to call by the first name. Usually in schools where the student is called out by the first name - remembers it throughout his life with comfort. Politicians make it a habit of calling people by their names. To gain goodwill, repeat the name of the person during a conversation trying to remember his features and appearance. This helps to remember the name easily. When you call by the name, the bond is closer. The person is happy to hear the name. Harry is a gymnasium instructor in Modern gym. The gymnasium owner is happy with Harry's work. For attracting new customers, he earns a commission which is double his salary. Starting a boy working as an instructor, it's been many years. He starts instructing men, within a week he calls each one of them by their names. People find this quite comfortable. They start enjoying exercise with Harry as if he was their childhood friend. After his job in the gymnasium on his way home, he meets people whom he addresses by their names. Interaction with a pleasing name is so appreciated. So people start joining the gymnasium for their workout. There is a positive mindset. People enjoy hearing their name. You release a magnetic force of attraction with the first name. Very few people do this. Calling the name of the employees helps to run a business well. The employee has a sound of his name soothing to the ears. He or she would work fast and put out good ideas with personal closeness to the development of the firm. He may feel comfortable to hear his name rather than the designation of a worker. People are proud of their names. Successful entrepreneurs, politicians, social workers usually use this pattern to gather their friends and followers.

In this chapter, we have just completed how to impact others with the energy; your presence radiates to inspire them. You get connected to people wherever you go, spreading huge ripples of hope, the assumption you make, the caring attitude you show your wholehearted support through the quality time shared.  Call everyone with the first name, it's pleasing. Your presence will help others feel empowered and calm to befriend you. In the next chapter, you learn to attract friends through your appreciation.

# Chapter 4 Admire the Good Qualities in People

William James said, "The deepest principle in human nature is the craving to be appreciated."

## Praise Good Qualities

All of us like the people who admire us. Appreciation is liked by all, so they are happy with the ones who appreciate. I recall a story I heard in my childhood. There was a village adjoining the forest. There lived a dacoit who had a daily routine of killing people after robbing them. He lived happily in the jungle linking two villages. One day he stopped a traveler. He threatened him, "Give all that you possess." The traveler said, "I have a few silver coins, which I don't mind sharing with you. Why are you doing this? You are a good creation of God. You have strong muscles, to bring awards in wrestling". "Hahaha", laughed the dacoit, "Are you giving the belongings or shall I kill you?" The traveler responded, "Think of a happy life, treat others well. You are a good human, so leave this bad habit." The second impact for this praise was pleasing. The dacoit was overwhelmed with this appreciation. He knelt, "Please suggest a new way of life that I can follow". He confessed to his crime and started a new life. The stranger had highlighted and triggered the good in him.

You go out to party with companions; appreciate the dress one is wearing, its design, the way she carries it, reflect your happiness in her beauty. There is a way you develop this skill of finding quality to appreciate others. Apply it regularly in life.  It keeps people around you. Friends can do a lot in your day to day life. Praise honestly with good intention.

My observations of a few years say that a key reason for divorce is the lack of appreciation. We often take our spouses so much for granted that we never appreciate them. The wife cooks food for the family and looks after the kids, despite having a day job. She maintains a good balance as if she has multiple hands. Her work needs appreciation. Thank her for the delicious food she cooks.  She has taken efforts for the family. Similarly, the husband works hard to win daily bread for the family. Maybe it is a 9 to 6 job, or a business. Every effort deserves praise. Welcome your spouse daily with words of admiration. Say, "Darling, welcome home. You look tired after a heavy work in the office; you surely did your best today." Your compliment is a boost to him or her. The tired mind is refreshed. You should have some softness and tenderness in you while speaking. Your family is a friend too.


**Praise the Improvement**

In a school, a child was not able to keep up with the class or show progress like his classmates. All students laughed at him and mocked him. His even attempting to do anything annoyed others However, his teacher was kindhearted. She praised him as he told the birthday of a classmate. He was overjoyed. He, after a week, mentioned the birthdays of all his classmates. The teacher lavishly praised and clapped for him. The class was surprised. They all praised this boy for his memory. The boy started memorizing his Math tables and recited poems. The change in his behavior was experienced by all. This happened due to praise.

The hard work, one's perseverance in achieving the goal - praise every bit of changes one makes in daily routine towards improving. A child aspiring to get into the topmost college of the state, crack the fellowship exam of a country, getting scholarships. It can be sports too. An athlete breaking his previous record, losing weight in pounds, reversing a lifestyle disorder. Going out for completing the bucket list. An emu ride, a marathon run, ballet dance, opera singing - there are multiple reasons for you to praise others for even simple moves.

Praise the work of your colleagues, your school, or college classmates daily. Praise children for small drawings, paintings, sketches, thread work, learning a mantra - just anything.

It is human nature to be happy and get encouraged with praise. Praise is an appropriate way to connect to people.

## Appreciate good qualities

"My best friend is the one who brings out the best in me."

Henry Ford

Whenever you meet any new person, find three good qualities in him. It can be his language, style of speaking, way of dressing, hairstyle, body language, or the way he carries himself. Then move on for further adding two more to them – his gestures, knowledge about the topic he is speaking, communication skills, etc. You can always find good in others to appreciate. Appreciation brings out the best in you. You avoid being envious and negative about the person. This will keep you away from criticism.

It is human nature to find faults with every physical appearance of a person at first sight. You try to see the other with your mindset. Your likes and dislikes are bestowed on that new personality, you dislike the orange color. A pretty girl with an orange outfit attends a party where you are invited. You start criticizing because you see her through your likes and dislikes. Don't heed to gossip as many do it very well with zero output. A gossipmonger gathers all false chatter-boxes. Do not think she has a costly dress that you don't possess. Instead, approach her to appreciate her designer outfit, her beautifully dressed hair, and how pretty she looks with the neckpiece. She will be happy with your appreciation. Fill yourself with positive vibes for her. She will remember you for your appreciation. You become a part of the most memorable moment. Next meeting she will approach you for a conversation.

In the office appreciate a new idea your colleague is working on. Avoid sulking enviously for others' achievements. Sim said, "Hello Jack, you got a big project to work on? Congratulations, you deserve it." Jack happily replied, "Yes quite a big one, needs a lot of effort with planning, will you help me? You're so good at it." Sim praised the good qualities in Jack without any hesitation. In return, she got to be a part of the project, which was her dream. She developed a good, friendly relation with Jack. They worked efficiently with proper coordination. Both efficiently completed the project. They were rewarded by the company. One can earn special respect for your friendship.

A classmate in college plays guitar well, appreciates that skill. "What melodious tunes you play! Are you learning since childhood?" You can start the praise, which is true. The classmate will be pleased to share his views about playing and learning the notes on the guitar. It is not everyone's passion to be a guitarist or a musician. Lots of efforts are put in to pluck the strings to the desired notes. A dancer on the dance floor has practiced long hours to be there. A singer practices for hours to perform for a large audience. A magician has practiced his tricks for hours together before you get to see his performance. These skills need time, perseverance, and consistency. Search skills in a person and appreciate them. A performer is satisfied with admiration from the audience. Classmates appreciated for their skills will befriend you easily. While hosting a large event, they will wait for your opinion to move on.

You are in a function. There are some performers - the dancer, the singer, the musician, the magician, etc. Appreciate their work. Meet the chef of the day to admire the quality of the food he has prepared. Talk to the host for a grand celebration organized perfectly. These days we have event managers to take care of everything, yet your appreciation makes a lot of difference for the people. If you are kind, they have you fixed in their minds.

Concluding here, the importance you need friends to keep your life exciting can only be understated. Some friends are with you in every walk of life. They develop a strong bond with you. Appreciation of the simplest form is necessary for a good relation. People try to seek your praise. Whether a kid, teenager, collegiate, or grown-up, elderly, rich or poor - all long for praise. A well-meant well intended praise does help catch up friends. This book will help you achieve a strong bond. Learn more to be successful in winning friends step by step through this book. I look forward to giving you the keys to seek the help of others. Read further how you do these through the examples I have illustrated. Enjoy reading as you proceed.

# Chapter 5  Politely and tactfully get the Cooperation of People

## Be Good at Conversation

We always want people to work according to our will; whatever ideas we have, we wish to implement without any interference. Suzy knitted woolen wear, a variety of cardigans, pullovers stockings, and caps. She called a designer to help her. She had to pay a huge amount to designers, marketing experts. The designer said, "Madam, I am busy for the next two weeks." Suzy had a thought in mind. She packed all her incomplete woolen ware. She approached the customers to enquire about the designs they would enjoy wearing. The customers gave her the designs they wanted. She knitted the designs and all the woolen wear was sold. This confidence of self idea works in every walk of life. Politeness in your conversation and a decent tact you use to impress customers, lead to progress.

My daughter had a lesson 'Seven Sisters' in her English subject. It described the seven states in North East India. I Said, "Would you like to visit one of the seven sisters that you have studied?" "Yes Mom", she was excited. I told my husband, she will learn better if she visits the place to see the culture. He liked the idea. Within a fortnight, my husband at breakfast announced a surprise for us. He said

"This year we are visiting Sikkim, one of the states mentioned in the 'Seven Sisters'.  One of the incredible places in India! It will be a study trip to the seven sisters." We had to have some destination for our visit during the vacation. My younger daughter was surprised at her dad's gift for the vacation. She was overwhelmed and excited to see a place described in the textbook. We began packing. A tactful way is always for the good of all. Such conversation tact can be useful in the workplace. Make one engrossed in the work of one's interest to get the best output in a friendly manner.

A similar way was used by a salesman, who very intelligently spoke to a real estate owner. He said, "Sir we are a company manufacturing lifts. Please do come to suggest the ones that your firm would need. Advise us on the pattern, for the convenience of your buildings. We will be obliged to serve you." The entrepreneur was delighted by this talk. He was very happy and excited at the thought that someone in another firm wanted his advice. He made a quick visit to the company to design suggestions for the lifts. He started recalling all necessities in a lift and studied the same on his way to the firm. Since his views and advice were taken into consideration, he wished to buy the lift for himself first. He booked four for his real estate within a couple of hours. He was impressed. It gave a good job to the salesman.

## Be a Good Listener

Listening needs a lot of patience. Most of the people like a person listening to them and not the one speaking. During functions, we try to avoid mighty-on speakers. To befriend, the best way is to smile and listen to the other.

Lend your ears to a friend in college. You can sit in the canteen or a coffee shop. Communicate with new pals, professors in college. Go in for two-way communication, but first listen carefully to the other person. Show you are interested in what he or she has to say. Make them feel you care for them, so are listening. Express as if you are listening such talk for the first time. Make them feel you are concentrating on their talk. Let that be any problem they're trying to solve or any difficulty they are facing.

Mrs. Jones had many friends in the residential colony. She made it a routine to spare time for the neighbors. She listened to her friends carefully with positive gestures, nodding her head. In the evening she sat in the common park for all to visit her for the talk. They revealed the success of children at school, the water level reduced in a dam, the supply of electricity, the green-grocer delivering fresh vegetables, whatever the topic was. She kept a lot of patience to hear about subjects out of interest for her. This helped her attract many helpful friends. She was a common friend to many and helped solve their daily issues. Any common decision was finalized with her consent.

Dr. APJ Abdul Kalam, the eleventh President of India, in his book 'The Turning Point' writes, 'One of the most beautiful sights I have seen, was in Sudan - that of the Blue Nile and the White Nile merging and being transformed into a different color'. In meeting people, we are transformed too. He was a good listener and conversed with the young generation of India. He loved to listen to children and answered their questions. He always found pleasure in interacting with the upcoming generation of the country.

I would like to tell you something about listening. Improve your listening skills; as when a person speaking with a long pause, he could divert your attention. It may bore you, but show that it is of great value to you. Listen carefully to the speaker, as it is his first conversation. Do not look around or do any other work of writing, typing, talking on a mobile phone. Look into the eyes of the speaker. Respond positively to the speaker. Make him feel comfortable with your gestures. Concentrate on his talk. Nod your head, smile in agreement. Increase his confidence with your gestures.

## Encourage others to Speak

The power of the language of friendship has immense meaning when one speaks. Let the person speak to release all stress or fear inside him; or the daily happenings in life such as pain, rejection, achievement, laughter. The unsaid, unread truth of life can be revealed. People just wait to have a friend to speak out all these emotions. Your encouraging them to speak is a heavy sigh of relief for them. Drain out their emotions through talking. Avoid any type of gossip; it leads to weakening your thoughts.

In college, if you want to befriend anyone, let him or her speak. Be it about college life, the village or countryside he or she comes from, or experiences in college. Always wait for the other to finish his words. Help the one who is facing any difficulty. Eliminate obstacles in their progress. Try to solve them by listening to every detail of the story. Proceed through legal means. Do not use any wrong ways to make one believe you are good. Ask questions to get to the right track. If you can do this for someone, that person will befriend you.

You are interested in sports, go to the gymnasium and watch your friends practice their game or exercise. Enquire about him and the practice hours. Encourage him to speak about his goals. Within four days, his eyes will start searching you in the gymnasium, on the ground. He will start sharing many experiences with you. How he started the game? Who encouraged him? What are the obstacles in his way? How he tries to overcome them? Get to know something new and beneficial every day.

One day I went for an outing with friends. One of them stated that she had a sleepless night. This was due to the delicacies she had relished for dinner, "Oh no! It was perhaps the ice-cream that I had. Wasn't it the anxiety of the outing as I had not been there?" She kept on talking about this throughout our journey. Julie was another extreme, a jolly girl. She kept on talking about all things positively. She said, "I was so excited about the journey to a new site. I had dinner early, said my prayers before going to bed, wished good night to all my family members, and cleaned my feet that had to work a lot the next day. I had a sound sleep to wake up fresh today."

## Have a positive attitude towards your talks.

Speaking about others' problems or achievements gives great relief to a person. You share your smallest success with a person who, you feel, will listen to you. If there is none to listen to, one is depressed. In India, at some places, there are public places for common water taps. Here there is a specific schedule for the municipality water supply. Women gather there to collect water and speak about their problems daily. They also come together for washing clothes, after doing the fieldwork, or at the common weekly market day.  This is how they befriend each other. This makes them happy. They eagerly wait to meet the mighty listeners. So the art to encourage others to speak is fulfilling in developing a good friendship that lasts long.

Let them speak about their financial problems. Be it a loan taken for a house, purchasing an article, study abroad, or educational loan. The check is perhaps bounced or the EMI is stuck up. Try to give space through verbal communication.

"Today you look very tired and unhappy. What's the reason?"

She replied, "I have the opportunity to study abroad but my father can't afford the expenses."

"Then let's go to search for a scholarship."

The person catches up the attention to speak out all details, for such politeness and a good ear; the positivity in the willingness to help doesn't go unnoticed.

You have decided to organize a large program which you have neither attended nor done in life. Meet people to talk it out to them. Chalk out the program in detail. Make a big framework for it. Consider every small aspect of the outcome. Plan the need and greed of the event. Tell people how they will be benefitted from it. The benefit may not be a financial gain all the time. It can be in any incentive - free counseling, book, talk, lecture, a movie, a small gift hamper that a rich too will love to carry home.  Let your talk be in terms of the interest of others so they start willingly working on it and happily cooperate you without any grudges.

**E speaking**

Talk through emails or social media. You can type a message in email and get into communication to develop friendships. Go through the profile of the desired candidate. A lot of chatting can be done through social media. Get to know about the passion, profession of the new pal before you extend your friendship. Just do not chat, but help your friend to overcome his difficulties. This can lead to a collaborative business establishment. There are many friends on social media like Facebook, Twitter, Instagram; you must first check their profile. Learn about them, and then proceed for friendship. These social media give you exposure to a wide variety of friends. The process you handle by sending effective messages, recorded videos of any information to gather people for your webinars, is quite enlightening. Have pals all around the globe. The easiest way for the shy ones is e-friendship. It takes your fame around the globe. That's the right manner to propagate your idea and establishment of creativity.

Here you can work for your progress, growth development, and dignity.

After reading this chapter you summarize that you can acquire some skills of talking to others, listening carefully to help one solve the problems. Acquaint to friends abroad through the internet, get friends through social media, and explore good business with assistance from them. Start something new to sow seeds of friendship to reap a good harvest in life. In the next chapter, I will teach you how to involve others in what you do by interesting them to do so.

# Chapter 6 Develop Interest of People in Your Work

Martin Luther King said, "Darkness cannot drive out darkness, only light can do that."

## Be enthusiastic

Express yourself to your colleagues. Your enthusiasm cheers others to work.  Involve them in your work. Clarify your ideas, as clarity is power. Become the light to remove the darkness from people's life.

Any task that you are given, divide it among your colleagues. Arouse their interest in your work. Allow them to work. Many may not like to do so. It can be as simple as conducting activity in a school, competition for upgrading your firm, developing popularity among the masses, etc. Plan the competition, distribute the work to collect the entries, conduct the competition, judging the participants, and give it as per their liking and capabilities. You can never satisfy all, but you can surely make them enthusiastic in their work. Be interested in your work to apply full energy without being exhausted. Find God in your friends and work to keep enthusiasm. "Speech is power. Speech is to persuade to convert, to compel. It is to bring another out of his bad senses into your good sense."

Tony Robbins, "To communicate, we must realize that we are all different in the way we perceive the world and use the understanding as a guide to our communication with others."

In South Asian countries, it is a tradition to fly kites during some festivals. It was a kite-flying season. There was a kite-making competition organized in the city, yielding high prizes. There were large hoardings erected at prominent squares in the city, as an encouragement to children to acquaint themselves with the tradition and enjoy the activity. Sham wanted to participate in the competition. He could make the kite but didn't have enough money to pay the entry fee. He went to a boy in his neighborhood.

Sham said, "Dinu, have you heard about the kite making competition in the city?"

Dinu replied, "Yes, but how do we get there?"

"Dinu, I will teach you to make the best kite you ever have seen. Do accompany me for the competition and fill half of the entry fee."

Dinu very happily agreed, "Yes, what a good idea of making a kite to win the competition! I will talk to mom and fill the entry fee soon. See you at the competition. Thanks a lot for choosing me as a companion."

Dinu learned a new skill of making a kite. Sham could participate in the competition by teaching his friend. Learn to gain mutual benefit by telling how he gets the benefit.

Try to speak in terms of benefit for the one before you. So that person is enthusiastically involved in your work, and joins happily and with fulfillment. Tell the take away for the person of the new scheme that you are launching. He will keep aside all the difficulties to be at your side for his interest. Involvement is for sure. Rosy, the owner of the villa, always greeted her tenants in the morning. While on a morning round towards the backyard, she said, "Hello, come out to enjoy the sunshine. You will enjoy a good day in the garden on planting some basil and enjoy taking care of your plants."

The children were happy to hear this. They began gardening along with Rosy. Soon a beautiful garden in the backyard was developed. The children ensured Rosy, early morning work in the garden. The children, within a few years, enjoyed the fruits of the trees they had planted in the garden.

Taking responsibility means you are growing to empower yourself.

Michael was working for a firm. He said, "Mary, we are working on a plan for tomorrow, I will get customers. You maintain their details on your PC."

She was excited, "Yes" she agreed, "Henry will speak to them."

Henry too joined in; he was the most impressive speaker in the firm. He was successful in his task with his friends and got cooperation from them. Thus all collaborated to get work done positively. Talk to people how you can be a help to profit them.

Your boss entrusts a job for you. You have never sent an email. You know nothing about the internet. Would you deny the project? Accept it as a challenge. There comes the opportunity to connect to people. Send your bait to gather your fish.

"If you can't communicate and talk to other people and get across your ideas, you're giving up your potential."

Warren Buffet

## Begin conversation

Self-confidence is very effective for the mind to start a talk. It is a foundational habit to begin a conversation with a big smile. Before you begin your conversation, smile. A real smile is the most powerful weapon to attract friends to win them. Avoid a fake smile, even a liar or a thief can smile at the sight of the police. Try to be genuine to interest the other in your talk. In a lavish party hosted by a millionaire friend, I was sitting with my kid at the table as others were at the bar. I found another lady in the same state. I walked up to her table and simply wished her a 'Hello'. She too greeted and invited us to join them at the table.

"You have a cute child," I remarked.

She had a pleasant smile on her face, "Thank you," she nodded pleasantly.

I inquired, "Are you a relative or a business associated guest?"

She very proudly replied, "A relative."

Here began the conversation among the ladies. It went on for quite some time with all the topics to discuss on earth. Now she's a good friend of mine. She is associated with me in my business too.

A collegiate can use the way to begin a conversation with the one he wants to befriend. Start with a "Hi, shall I help you with the books to the library?"

You'll often get a 'yes' reply. Try to find if a musical instrument, a bag, or anything else other than books to begin with. If you start the conversation, you can have your topic for discussion - the weather, the natural beauty of the place, the current political situation, books, and authors, the reality of life, sports, the college campus, etc. The secret to making people like you is to make them realize how much you care for them. Let intelligence flash through your eyes. That will catch the attention of a sports personality towards you. Converse in such a way, that he looks forward to meeting you.

## Be Funny

Make jokes and be funny. Comedians have the skill to crack jokes. You can develop this skill. People love to watch comedy shows, live or recorded. It helps to distract from sorrow and stress. Listening to and seeing funny acts relaxes one. You capture the attention of friends in high school or college quickly if you crack jokes. Have humor in your interactions. At school, friendship is just companionship. Sometimes your funny nature drags all towards you. Be clear to get a positive and true one. Both girls and boys must think of the society around them to get a funny attitude. It is a skill that can be acquired. Leave the spark of your intelligence to crack a joke on the spur of the moment.

## Be curious

"The important thing is not to stop questioning. Curiosity has its own reason for existing."

Albert Einstein

A small child is full of curiosity, wants to know everything about the smallest article like a new bag, a ball or a big laptop, air-filled in a balloon, the parachute. The child wants to touch it, scroll the screen, play games, find the paint keys, word art, even jump from a parachute, or fly in the air. Apply the same curiosity to know a stranger to help in your task. There's a new employee in your office, reach out to him to find out his skills. Let the curiosity in you enhance to develop an interest in other's work. Cultivate a habit of curiosity. It is a form of self-improvement.

## Inquire

Stimulate the creativity of your colleague by asking questions. He may not like you directly ordering him. This makes it easy to understand your order. He takes it as a casual question to begin his work. He will cooperate with you in the future too. It develops a healthy friendship. The person will be happy to do the work you tell. This tact may always not be very pleasing for the other person. He can work as he knows the skill or is his hobby. You can get your work done easily.

Quench the thirst for knowing a person by asking questions. Find what he is good at, his skills, hobbies, etc that could be useful, to involve him in your work. You have to ask the other person to show his skill to get your work done. After work, meet your neighbors at least once a day. Inquire about their health or any problems they face.

The walls in my colony had to be painted. Youngsters were asking if anyone could do so. Rajesh said, "I have inquired about the tenant's hobby, it is painting. Let us assign the work to him."

The work was assigned to Vijay, the tenant. The task developed good relations among the colony members and an outsider. Be an inspiring friend that all would like to treasure.

Communicate with your values and expectations. Be clear about your resentment.

At the end of this chapter, you have learned that to be friends, one you have to begin talking, manifest your potentials, have a questioning spirit, and be inquisitive to know more about new people. Have a nature to be funny, happy; take the lead, and be responsible for activities. Communicate well to catch up with the attention of others. While you communicate, overcome the habit of annoyance to check the mistakes. A sensible and effective way is to communicate fearlessly. Practice the technique of suggestions. You will learn this technique as you read the last chapter of this book.

# Chapter 7 Correct Mistakes Easily

## Smile

Smile increases your face value. Use a smile as an asset.  On a trip to Goa with family, I visited various churches there. In one of them, there were small stalls. On the way to the exit door, there was a small library. Some people were selling books, key chains, bracelets, wristbands, etc. My daughter, very small then, tried to touch one of the books. The young salesgirl, with a beautiful smile on her face, slapped my daughter's hand. She quickly withdrew her hand off the book. My daughter learned a good lesson to remember throughout her life. You can help your friends to improve with this technique.

Your smile allows being comfortable to overcome the erring part. The person will check several times once your smile tells her there is a correction essential. It will be accepted with ease rather than condemn, angry words, resistance, or abusive language. A smile will cool the mind.

## Avoid Arguments

Sir Isaac Newton's third law of gravitation states that every action has an equal and opposite reaction.

The best way to correct someone is through diplomacy. Do not try to prove that someone is wrong. Even welcome the disagreement. Learn to think over your opponent's ideas, so that you learn every small bit of it. Try to persuade the one before you. Arguments waste time, and the negative energy spoils relations and goodwill. Speak in a polite and non-aggressive way. You should avoid reacting to others' mistakes in a sarcastic, revengeful manner. You are responsible for your anger. Try to control it for gathering a hive of friends to collect nectar.

Arguments lead to negativity in thought that weakens you. It creates unnecessary bad circumstances for all. Do not try to win an argument. In the evening every day, I visit the square of the colony in my residential area. With a few friends, I sit there to spend fifteen minutes. There are people moving out for a walk or jog, some are returning from their offices. One day a person from among them invited us for a ritual. My friend and I visited the professor's house. She was delighted to see us. A welcome drink was served. The professor started with her experience of the work, she was awarded for. We got into a conversation soon. The professor said, "I visited the western coast of India to see the shipbuilding industry at Vishakhapatnam.

"O yes, Vishakhapatnam is a lovely place", I replied.

My friend wanted to tell her that the place is on the east coast, looked at me with annoyance. I smiled back at her. There was a lot of discussion on shipbuilding at various places in the world.  We left the house.

My friend remarked, "How can you tolerate the wrong location of a place?"

I replied, "The professor was very happy for our first visit to her house. The location of a place was not a matter of our subject. We don't have to win over her by any argument. We had to be friendly to establish a good friendship with a new member".

My friend realized, "That's right, one can do that to win a view."

"He who wants to persuade should put his trust, not in the right argument, but at the right word. The power of sound has always been greater than the power of sense."

Joseph Conrod

## Do not Insult

Speak politely, without being angry or using harsh words. This is one of the most difficult tasks one has to perform. It comes with practice. You keep worrying about a mistake one has done, but that person is enjoying life. Do not offend his enjoyment. Do react nicely to rudeness. No problems can make one miserable, other than one's own thoughts. Your attitude of looking at the other should change.

In a confectionary, Adam, the manager, was always a perfectionist at work. He scolded and insulted his coworkers every while. All were unhappy bringing down the performance; this affected the sale of the unit. Sony, my friend, wanted to close down the confectionary. She discussed it with me.

I replied, "Find the root cause of the dullness of the workers in the unit."

I went on a visit. As I approached the baking section with a big set up of ovens, I was astonished to find Adam howling at Mona, "You stupid girl, can't you see I am here yet no salute from you?"

The poor girl stood shivering and confused, with tears in her eyes. She was speechless.

"Sony, I have an answer to your problem," I said.

After the lunch break, I requested her to schedule a meeting with Adam. I greeted Adam with a big smile to make him feel at home. I began, "Look Adam you are managing the confectionary very well that one can never think of someone else for this job."

Happily, he replied, "Thank you, Ma'am."

I continued, "For improving the yield of the unit, I wish you all work with a happy mindset. Smile and politely point out the mistakes of the workers."

"Yes madam," he agreed. He started the change in his behavior. Within three months, Sony visited me with a big box of cake to celebrate the remarkably increased turnover of her confectionery.

## Encourage to accept the faults and correct them easily

My niece took up a drawing class with a teacher. The teacher would say, "You are too slow to complete the drawing. You will not achieve anything at this sluggishness."

She was demoralized. She quit drawing. Six months later my cousin enrolled her in a new drawing class. The teacher set a time challenge for her, beginning with drawing an apple in fifteen minutes, and then coloring it in the next fifteen minutes.

Trying to overcome the challenge, she began, "Throw away your old outdated method. Accept the new way."

With such new empowering words of her teacher, my niece began to love drawing. She grew up to be an artist, and now exhibits her drawings in art galleries. She treasures her teacher as a friend. The first exhibition was inaugurated at an elderly friend's hand.

Use this formula to gain friends through encouragement. Easy to accept a faulty way and correct it.

## Forgive

Forgive the one who made you angry. It will make you strong with higher energies. It decreases the goodness in you. Count to ten, so that time dilutes your anger. Interact with others with forgiveness. Remain relaxed to forgive others for your progress in being friendly. Let forgiveness be always there in your mind.

Try to understand and forgive. In a team game, this works fine to get friendlier. A team event can be successful when in an organized state. The hockey, football, basketball, cricket games have a big team involving at least ten to fifteen players, including the reserved. For a school in the town, it is easy as all belong to the known environment. If a district has to form a team, the first thing is to establish friendship to develop team spirit among the players. This is indeed a really difficult task. Players from all over the nation, belonging to different strata, environment, and states join in for the team game. Forgiveness over time helps to increase friendly relations. Forgive small mistakes. Overlook them. This will increase your confidence to be the number one team. The principle not only works for sports but also for any other achievement to take you to the topmost level. To realize the full potential in you, be friendlier through forgiveness.

School going kids also befriend with forgiveness. This has to be imbibed in them if not an instinct. Somu used to steal erasers and pens from others' bags. This had become his habit. All were searching who it could be.

Jonny said, "Somu I know you have stolen that pen. I won't reveal it to anyone if you quietly keep it back."

Somu agreed, "Ok Jonny."

Jonny forgave Somu and they were friends hereafter. Somu cultivated good habits with Jonny by his side.

When I studied in college, there were elections held for us, to understand political science and civic sense. Usually, two parties contesting the elections divided the students into groups. Youngblood always went for the extreme decisions. During the elections for the General Secretary (a post for students to be elected by the students from among themselves as a representative) of the college, there arose small quarrels. These then blew up to involve hockey sticks. It injured many innocent students, creating a fearful environment. Escalating further, police had to be involved. The act of forgiveness and kindness became the essence of life to curb these quarrels to gain friends.

# SUMMARY

You have read a simple formula to live a better life. Believe to practice it in your life to gather a honeycomb of friends throughout your life. The positivity, intention, and desire to help you acquire good friends to treasure - are my intentions through this book. Read again the main aspects to implement in your life. Increase your potential to interest people in your work. I have given some examples, written short stories to help you understand through the situations where you can create the opportunity to cultivate friendship. I am confident that you make use of the knowledge you got in reading this book, conquer your fears to speak confidently. As you enjoy reading now, it's time you practically use it to develop your personality. Lead a successful life with a big friend circle. Friends are a source of a healthy life. Speak all the evens and odds to them and remain happy. They share both your good and bad times. Parents can develop an informal friendship with their children. Spend quality time with them. Do not argue or hold any grudges over petty issues. Through respect, forgiveness, and tolerance you become a popular person caring for every small thing. Make assumptions; be optimistic to grow in abundant friendship. Online friendship can be achieved by initiating conversation through emails, Facebook, twitter. Generosity as well as your inclination to appreciate or praise one honestly and authentically will supply you with infinite friends.

Smile to reflect the higher energy in you, to forgive others, to begin a conversation. Control your anger, this will refrain you from insulting others. Insult weakens the mindset, which leads to discomfort. Do not criticize or condemn anyone. Frequently praise for even small improvements - whether small or big, rich or poor, it is human nature to aspire for praise. You are a unique person for inspiring others. Your creative and expansive energy drives you to acts of kindness. Be jocular, curious; keep asking questions, seeking advice to develop a friendship. This book will give you the ability to improve your skill to be with people, practice them even if you may find the suggestions practically difficult initially. Maintain a sheet to enroll friends from various fields you acquire. Connect with people to make them feel important, involving them in your work tactfully. You learn all the essentials to win friends in society. Just start according to this book, revise it to remain obstacle-free. Enjoy the company of your new friends, and start a new pattern in your life. There are several features explained to skillfully grow emphasis in present-day life. Use this book as a handbook of your daily life events. Make a sheet to record your behavior for not violating the important suggestions given to you. It will improve your ability to meet and deal with people.